Douglife's Guide to Dominating Local Search

Doug Montgomery

Contents

Forward

Introduction - 9
What is Local Search? - 13
Google Places - 17
Google Ranking - 22
Claiming Your Google Listing - 28
Adding Your Business to Google Places - 32
Getting the Most From Your Listing - 39
Reviews - 41
Other Google Services - 44
Other Important Local Listings - 49
Geo Target Your Photos - 58
Citations - 61
Advanced Techniques - 64
Facebook - 70
Spying on Your Competition - 72
On Page SEO for Local Business - 75
Conclusion - 77

Epilogue

Forward

There's no denying that the internet has changed the way we all do business.

It's no longer enough to place ads in newspapers, or advertise on radio, or place an ad in the yellow pages. With over 76% of Americans turning to the internet for their product and service searches, it's important for any business to make the internet a crucial part in their marketing strategy.

I've spent most of my professional career in the IT field, growing along with the computer age on into the World Wide Web. And during this time, I've seen how the online evolution has changed the landscape of marketing for local businesses, and I've seen it successfully catapult businesses to prosperity and success.

But in order for this to happen with your business, you need to know the right way to use the internet to successfully market your business. If you don't take advantage of using the web to market your business, then you stand the chance of being left in the dark while your competitors take the lion share of the online business away from you.

In this book I will show you how you can effectively use the internet to find more customers, increase your sales, and dominate your local search marketing landscape. I will share with you the marketing secrets and strategies that I have used with my own clients time after time to help them achieve their business goals and dreams.

A Great Business Website is Just the Beginning but Crucial

Since 2001, I've built hundreds of professional websites for clients all over the world. I've had my hands in everything from direct marketing landing pages to complete brand creation for some of the biggest names in entertainment and product sales. And I certainly believe your website is the first critical component in your online professional image.

But even the best, most professional website will do you no good if no one knows it exists, or can see it. You must take measures to spread the word and help potential customers find your website and ultimately buy your products and/or services.

I'm sure you've heard of SEO by now, but if you haven't, let me quickly outline it for you. SEO, or Search Engine Optimization, is a paid or free method used to bring traffic to your website. It is a proven fact that ranking well with Google or Bing can drive large amounts of traffic to your website. SEO is the on-site and off-site modifications you can do to improve your visibility within Search Engines. If you plan on achieving long-term success with your business, you need to invest time and money into Online Marketing and particularly Search Engine Optimization.

Google is the largest, most popular search engine on the internet today. Over 70% of people searching for local businesses turn to Google first. They do their research online first by going from website to website before they buy. They'll judge your business first by the professional look of your website. Then they'll judge your products and services by the website content you've made available to see if you have what they are looking for.

I wrote this book to help business owners better understand how to best use Google for their local business marketing. By the time you finish reading this book, you will have the tactics and knowledge you need to get your business noticed online in Google Places.

Let's get started on your journey to online success!

Doug Montgomery

NOTE: The internet is ever-growing, ever-evolving and Google is constantly making changes and modifying how they present your local business in their search results. This book reflects my best practices and procedures as they are at this time. I will continually update this information to keep pace with ongoing changes. And I will make these updates available to you.

To receive updates from me on this book, just send an email to doug@douglife.com with "update" in the subject line and I'll keep you informed of changes as they become available.

Greetings!

When someone types the name of a product, service, or company into an Internet search engine, hundreds of pages of relevant data is displayed to help the consumer find what they're looking for.
If your business is not listed on the first or second page of the search results, your customers may never find you.

Simply put, Google is the new "yellow pages." With Google being used for over 70% of all internet searches, it makes sense that every local business should concentrate their internet marketing efforts on Google.

And, if your business can't be found on the first two pages of Google, then you're basically invisible on the internet, because 87% of Google searches do not make it past the bottom of Google's first page.

Your Google+ Business listing will give your business the online visibility it deserves. When you have a business listing that has been approved by Google+ and when consumers type in specific keyword phrases, your listing will display from your Google+ Business listing no matter the browser or device!

This book will show you how easy it is to dominate your local competition with a fully optimized Google+ Business listing along with a few other juicy tidbits of advice.

This book will also walk you through the steps needed to optimize your Google Places and Google+ Pages through several techniques that work together to create a great foundation for you to start with.

The power of these techniques comes from using the entire process rather than just implementing a portion of them... and while you can skip some of the seemingly small techniques that make up part of this strategy, it will subtract from the dominance you gain by not using all of the steps together.

Jumping Right In

SEO can be costly and time consuming if you're un-informed...and in my opinion not a great place for local businesses to spend their time (or money). SEO is a moving target that changes dramatically all the time, literally shaking things up and turning the search results upside down on a regular basis. With Google being the large shareholder of searches at 67% in 2012, many businesses find the "quick solution" to SEO only fails for them as time progresses, creating even more work than before as they struggle to appease the "Search Gods".

With that being said, having a solid SEO strategy is not out of the question and can be a great way to increase sales, but it requires planning, research, and a good level of execution to be a success, which in this current economy, that's something many small businesses just don't have the resources available to do so.

However, if you own a business that relies on a customer base in your local area, let's say within a 50 mile radius, then Google provides several advantages for advertising your business and reaching your customers.

Here's a few worth mentioning:

- Mobile Devices rely heavily on Local Listings

- Google Places is and will always be free.

- Your business listing can appear on the first page of a particular Google search if optimized correctly.

- You can offer discounts and coupons for one day, one week, or one month.

- Your website, physical mailing address, and your phone number are displayed in your listing, which allows customers to find you more quickly and to get the information they need. (Especially on Mobile Devices)

- You don't need a physical retail or warehouse location to get verified by Google+. (This guide will show you how to get approved.)

Taking Advantage of Local Search

As a local business, you have a huge opportunity to dominate your local competition by getting a prominent listing at the top of search engines, using Google's local search features. Google has spent a large investment on becoming the most relevant search engine to its users and this book is your secret weapon for local businesses to climb to the top of Google search results in your area.

Local Search is the key to your online success... and this book is your key to getting your business listed on top of Google's local search.

The information I share in this book is the same information that I follow for my clients, who consistently pay me hundreds of dollars and monthly maintenance to keep their business at the top of Google's search results...and it's the exact same information I share in my 4-figure marketing seminars.

I did not write this book to promote Google+ or Google, but instead to help you dominate your competition in your local area by using what I know works. If you follow my steps as laid out in this book, it will teach you how to open the online floodgates of more business through the internet.

Chapter 1

WHAT IS LOCAL SEARCH?

Whenever you perform a search on Google, your search results often include a local area map and several local business listings. The local listings are prominently identified by map markers next to each of those listings.

Google primarily determines if a search is local based on these factors:

1. The searcher uses a geographic reference in their search: instead of a search for "dentist," the searcher includes a location like "Inverness Dentist" or "dentist in Inverness."

2. Google uses your IP to determine your location and returns results based on that location combined with the search query.

So Google either identifies your search as originating from a specific place, or the search itself includes a Google local search category for that geographic area. These results come from the Google Maps database.

When you do a search for a "place" that includes a "business category" recognized by Google, it returns local businesses listings relating to your search. More importantly, these results are almost always at the very top of the search results!

Studies have shown over and over again that being at the top of Google means more traffic, more exposure, and more business. And if you own a local business, this is where you want to be. In the days when the yellow pages were the dominating "go to" source for finding local businesses, this top Google maps listing is the equivalent to a full color, full page phonebook ad.

Local search is often categorized as a search being made with the intention on finding something (business, product, service) in a specific geographic area. More specifically, local online searching often leads to a transaction or purchase that eventually happens offline in a business' physical location.

More simply put, if you live in San Francisco and you do an online search for a plumber or a pizza, the search engines understand that you want to find a plumber or pizza in the San Francisco area—not somewhere else. And because the search engines know where you are (based on your device's IP address) they can now display the most relevant local information for your search term.

In an effort to provide the most relevant information to you, local search has become of great importance to the search engines.

Here's why:

Fact: Nearly All Consumers (97%) Now Use Online Media to Shop Locally. (BIA/Kelsey and ConStat , 2010).

Quite simply, the name of the game for the search engines is RELEVANCY. And the search engine that can be the most relevant will likely be the most used search engine...and where the eyeballs go, so does the advertising dollars.

Needless to say, over the past few years Google has become and remained the most dominant search engine on the planet. And I would argue that this for no other reason than the simple fact that Google usually returns the most relevant information for any given search term.

The biggest concern of Google is to be the most relevant search engine to their users. This comes first to Google. Being the most relevant makes Google the "go to" search engine on the planet. Being the "go to" search engine means more customers, which in turn, makes them the "go to" source for advertisers.

I have seen people who have tried to "out-think" or "out smart" Google, in an attempt to make Google see their website or advertisement as "relevant" when it really was not. Google takes no nonsense from suspected scammers who try to "mess" with their system as many saw in 2012 with the Panda & Penguin Algorithm updates.

The point I am trying to make is that Google strives first to be the most relevant. Making money comes next (naturally) after being the most relevant. For purposes of this book, you need to think "relevance" first—just as Google does. When you first try to be the most relevant to your customers, Google will reward you with higher rankings.

With over 70% of the online users using Google for their searches, this book will focus on getting your business at the top of Google—specifically with the use of Google Places, Google+ and Reviews.

Chapter 2

Google Places er..Google+ Pages!

Google Places is a revolutionary online service that can literally catapult a small, local business from obscurity to profitability almost overnight. By taking advantage of a Google Places listing (Now Google+ Pages), you can highlight your business' products and services and place your information in front of thousands of local customers who are searching for your particular type of business in your particular local area via numerous Google created areas online.

Not only will a listing on Google Places make your business stand out among dozens (sometimes hundreds) of local competitors, you will also get to tell potential customers a little bit about your business, obtain reviews, offer specials and other unique characteristics that your competition cannot.

Because your competitors may not know about Google Local or may not know the best way to optimize their Google Places listing to get top ranking on Google, this book will serve as your "secret weapon" to gaining a stronghold in your local market—a weapon to not only getting a free, Google Places listing for your business but also inside tips, tricks and secrets to securing a front page listing for your business so that your potential customers are finding you, and not your competition, when they conduct a Google search for your particular products and services in your area.

I've been involved with the internet and the SEO business since 2001. And many SEO "experts" will tell you that SEO is a highly complex and technical field. But with the introduction of Google Places for local searching, local SEO has become a lot easier and it makes more sense for local businesses to concentrate their efforts primarily on Google instead of worrying about all the other search engines out there.

In this book, I will show you how to claim your Google Places listing and then how to optimize your Google+ Page so that you—not your competition—are found first when your customers look for your products and services on Google.

In April 2009, Google announced that Local Search would start to show up more regularly in the "regular" search engine results pages, and since then, Google has delivered. Now, when you type in "plumber" or "pizza," Google serves up prominent, top of the page local listings that are relevant to your search terms.

Prior to Google Local, many businesses paid a fortune on Pay Per Click (PPC) ads to promote their businesses locally. Since Google Places came along, however, online advertising costs for local businesses were able to be dramatically minimized by replacing

PPC with a prominent Google Places listing. In my opinion, a Google Places listing is a much more effective way for local businesses to advertise on the internet than is their paid advertisement counterparts (on the right side of the Google page). Additionally, Google Places listings give many local businesses an opportunity to compete with their deep-pocketed competitors who could afford to pay for expensive PPC ads.

When your business is listed in Google Places, it will show up on the map feature when a local searcher (in your area) does a search for your business' products and/or services. The Google Map listing (local business results) is very bold and they stand out like a colorful "sore thumb" on the Google search results.

On November 7th 2011, Google launched Google+ Pages for Businesses and Brands which allowed businesses & brands to join Google social network.

Google+ Pages is more than just a name change. Instead, Google+ Pages offers even more tools to local business owners to increase their visibility online. There are currently two types of pages on Google for single businesses. These pages can be either:

- Place Page: Similar to the old format with scores and reviews
- Google+ Page: Will have all the social features provided by Google in addition to some other cool features rolling out

NOTE: Google+, like every business, has their rules and policies that they expect everyone to abide by. In that regard, Google does not approve business listings in every country in the world.

Therefore, before you attempt to create a business listing for yourself or your clients, it's important that you find out if Google+ is available in your area.

Chapter 3

Ranking within Google

How Google calculates search results and relevancy is a well-kept algorithmic secret and is purposely changed by Google on a constant basis. Google keeps tightlipped about their specific algorithms and the way they operate. But what I share here is based on my proven findings, testing, research and study.

As mentioned before, your business will benefit by being relevant in Google's eyes. The more relevant your business appears—the better rankings your business will get on Google Places. The key to this book is to show you what makes your business more relevant to Google.

Trust is a major factor that Google takes into consideration when ranking your business in search results. So, the likely question that comes to mind is, how do you go about gaining Google's trust.

When you verify your business with Google+ Business Listings, you go through either a telephone or snail mail verification. This must be done as your first step in gaining Google's trust. But while this is a step in the right direction, it is not going to give you automatic credit above your competition. You need to do more.

Business Website: A website is not required to be listed on Google+ Pages, but having a locally based website with search terms that are locally based for your business will surely factor in ranking your business on Google+ Pages.

Other Directories: Being listed in vertical, local, top tier and 2nd tier directories will be a major factor in Google's trust in your business. With listings in other directories, Google's trust in you will be greatly enhanced, as you will appear more likely to be a "real" business.

Reviews: It is hard to determine how much of a role reviews play in ranking your local business in Google Places, but reviews do play a factor. In my experience, the more reviews you have, the more trust Google will give you. This trust seems to relate to ranking as well.

Citations: Citations are mentions about your business on other websites. In traditional SEO, to rank higher in the search engines, it is imperative to have links that link back to your website. The more quality, relevant backlinks you have linking to your website, the higher you will rank. With local search, citations take the place of links.

There is more to creating a relevant Google+ Pages listing. Prior to creating your listing, you should research thoroughly three categories of key information. Once you have this written down, the rest of the process will go much faster.

The three research categories are:

1. Keywords
2. Competing businesses
3. Sponsored ad results

Keywords

Keywords and keyword phrases are the words that someone would type into a search engine to find a product, service, or company.

Step One: There are many free keyword tools available to you online, including the external Google keyword tool. But the fastest way to do your research is to open your favorite browser and type in the words that you would use when searching for a product or service that your business sells.

Step Two: Here's the important part, so pay attention. Not every keyword or keyword phrase will generate a Google+ Pages listing. Your job is to type relevant keywords into a search engine, and then see which keywords generate a Google+ Pages listing. You may very well have to do this a number of times until a map marker listing appears.

Step Three: Be sure to write down the keywords and keyword phrases that generated Google+ Pages listings. You will need those keywords when you create your business listing.

Competing Businesses

Since Google Places helps people find your business through local search results on both Google Search and Google Maps, it's important to know who your competition is so that you can stay ahead of them.

Here are two quick methods for staying ahead of your competition:

1.) When viewing the first page results on Google for a specific keyword, it's important that you look at the hyperlinked titles and descriptions of those businesses that were not listed in Google Places. Click the link and look at the home page of their website.

If a main keyword phrase for a business is "fish and chips", that keyword phrase is most likely used in the title, a description, and several times in the content of their home page.

Compare what you see after viewing the top 10 organic listings with the information contained on your website. Although there are more factors involved in getting to the first page of Google, you will now have an understanding of those businesses that are competing with you.

2.) Now what you need to do is to look at the top five listings in Google+ Pages. Click on each link and look at the information that is provided to someone searching for "fish and chips." You might want to print out each of those pages as a reference for when you're creating your Google+ Pages listing.

The reason this is important is because those companies have achieved top positions in Google Local Results. You can learn from their listings.

Study them; see what you can add to your listing later on. But whatever you do, do not cut-and-paste the exact words that another business has used to achieve their ranking in Google Search Results. That's called plagiarism and it's a punishable crime.

Sponsored Ads

If sponsored ads appear on the first page of Google for the keyword that you have selected, read their ads, and see if they're using the same keywords that you use for your business.

Sponsored ads indicate that business owners are spending money to place those ads for that chosen keyword. If you don't see any sponsored ads, it might be a good way for you to advertise your business in the future.

You can find out who your competition is if one company has a sponsored ad, along with a first page organic listing, and they're also included in the Google Places listing on the first page.

Study their listings. Visit their websites. See what you can learn and apply it to your own website, or your Google+ Pages listing.

The research and information that you uncover by performing these three processes will launch your business ahead of many other companies.

It will give you better placement, and doing a little upfront research will mean less work for you in the future to maintain your high ranking with Google Local Search.

Chapter 4

Claiming Your Google Listing

Before you do anything else, you need to find out if your business has already been claimed on Google+ Business Pages. This is something you or someone in your business would have to have done because it does require you to go through a confirmation process. Until recently, Google only allowed confirmation by mail. But now, they offer instant verification via callback service right to the telephone number you select.

Understand that your business may be able to be found on Google, but that does not mean the same as being "listed" with Google+ Business Pages. The fact that you can do a search for your business name and see 10,000 results showing up that contain your business name, does not mean your business has been claimed. Many make this mistake and tell me, "Oh, my business is already on Google, when in fact, it is not listed with Google+ Business Pages.

So, let's see if your business has been claimed...

Here's the method I use for all my clients and my own business as well. It's a quick and easy way to see if your business has been claimed or not for a few of the major directories. It even provides you with a score relative to your business on the Internet in terms of being officially listed or "claimed" in those directories.

Simply go to this website: http://www.getlisted.org

As you will see, this site is pretty self-explanatory. All you need to do to see if your business has been claimed is to type in your business name and the zip code to where your business is physically located.

As an example, I randomly typed in "Beverly Hills Plastic Surgery" with a zip code of "90210." A business was found under this name. But, this cosmetic surgery business has not claimed their Google Local listing (nor Yahoo, Bing, etc). This particular Plastic Surgery Business is leaving a great deal of money on the table by not having their business listing claimed.

Also, you will see that getlisted.org gives you a "listing score." In this case, getlisted.org assigned "Beverly Hills Plastic Surgery" a score of "0%" because the business has failed to claim a listing online.

Keep in mind that the higher the score, the better for your business as it is more likely to show up when people in your area are searching for your products and services.

This again goes to show you that your business may be found on Google but not be listed in Google+ Business Pages or Google Maps.

This means that when someone in the Beverly Hills area types "plastic surgery" or similar related search terms like "breast augmentation," "liposuction" etc, this business is not as likely to show up in Google+ Business Pages /Google Maps.

If our particular cosmetic surgeon had a copy of this book, he would easily be able to dominate this Google Map listing by knowing the secrets that you are about to learn.

Now, we will walk through getting listed in step-by-step fashion using a fictional business name.
Step 1: Go to getlisted.org and enter your business name and zip code.
Step 2: Next click the "Check My Listings" box.

Step 3: From here, we will click "Add your business listing" that appears on the Google logo at the top of the page.

Note: While this book focuses on Google, it is important that you add your business with as many listings as possible. By registering with each one, Google will look at your listing as being more relevant and trustworthy, which is very important in your rankings.

Chapter 5

Adding Your Business to Google+ Pages

You can now get started setting up your business listing to Google+ Pages. Now, if you already have a Google Places page, you can easily merge it or upgrade it by going to it and following Google's prompts. For those of you who haven't, let's begin by getting the proper items in order.

You will need:

- A Google Email Account (use one associated with your business and that can be shared with others such as assistants and service providers.)
- Basic Business Info (i.e. Name, address, phone number, URL, etc.)

Step 1: Go to http://google.com/places

Click "Get Started Now"

Step 2: Log into your Google account.

Step 3: Add a business.

To get started, simply click the "List your business" button. If you have more than one business you'd like to add but this is your first time going through the process, we recommend that you go through the steps with one business to familiarize yourself with the steps and information required. After that, you may choose to use the bulk upload option.

Important: Every line and field in the basic information page MUST be filled in with accurate information to make sure your site gets approved and indexed.

Step 4: Add your country and phone number.

Select your country from the dropdown. Add your phone number and click the "find business info" button to collect information already available about your business. This is based on your phone number so there may not be any info available.

Step 5: Add basic information.

In this step, you will add business information which includes your:

- **Country** – Select from dropdown
- **Company Name** – List exactly as you would a brick and mortar business
- **Street Address** – P.O. boxes are not allowed
- **City, State, Zip** – You will have the option to hide this info and set a service area in the next step.
- **Main Phone Number** – This should be the number to your business. It is best to use a local phone number rather than an out-of-state or toll-free one. Local customers will recognize local phone numbers quicker, and it is important for Google to deliver relevant information in the search results.

- **Email address** – This should be your support or public contact email address.
- **Website URL** – If you don't have a website, check the "no website" box. However, to get the best results, it's recommended that you have a business website.
- **Description** – This field is critical to your listing. Using your targeted keywords, write a clear and focused description that provides the most complete information you can about your business. NOTE: Remember to include your target keywords in your description. You may enter up to 200 characters.
- **Category (up to five)** – You must choose at least one from the list of categories offered in the dropdown. (Hint: The dropdown shows categories related to the first word you type in.) If you offer business to business services such as a virtual assistant, begin by typing "business or assistant" or one of the main keywords related to your industry.

Step 6: Define your customer service type.

- In this step, you will define your customer service type by answering a question about where your customers or clients receive services.
- If you have a local business where customers or clients come to the address you are listing, you will choose the first option – "No."
- If you operate an online business from home, that does not require customers or clients come to the address, choose the second option – "Yes."

Step 7: Select your service area and location settings.

As we said earlier, if you operate an online business from home and customers or clients do not come to the address you provided earlier, you may want to hide that address from your listing. To do that, just click the check box next to "Do not show my business address on my Maps listing."

Next, you will select your service area by distance or by list of areas served.

Service Area By Distance

When using the distance option supply your location (actual address, city only, or state only) and then choose the number of miles or kilometers around that area. In the example below, we chose the state of Tennessee and the surrounding 625 miles. Note: 625 is the maximum number allowed.

Service Area By List

If you'd like to choose a larger or more specific area, you may choose to define your service area by a list of specific addresses, zip codes, cities, or states/provinces.

(Hint: To choose the continental US, add the 4 corner states of Washington, California, Maine, and Florida – WA, CA, ME, and FL, respectively. You may also add other areas such as the provinces of Canada. Obviously, your service area will differ depending on your location and country.)

Step 8: Add your office hours.

Let people know when you're operating hours or when you're open for business. Just edit the days and times when you're open and closed.

Step 9: Add the payment options available to your customers.

Include your payment options for potential customers or clients who prefer to pay in a certain way.

Step 10: Add photos and videos to your Google Places page.

Add up to 10 eye-catching photos from your computer or from an online folder. Make sure you hold the copyright for these. To add an image from your computer, click the "Browse" button to search for images. Then click the "Add Photo" button to upload.

If you want to use an image, which you already have uploaded online, choose the "photo from web" option and add the URL of the image. Then click "Add Photo."

If you have a business related video on YouTube, you may add up to 5 URLs here.

The more information you can add to your listing, the more complete and more details Google will have to work with when determining search results.

Step 11: Add other details that your customers would find helpful.

Add other details, which make you stand out in the crowd for potential customers or clients such as parking, brands or product types you carry, etc.

Step 12: Submit Info

Double check the info you've added and click the submit button to create your listing.

Step 13: Confirm your location.

Depending on your country and location, you may have two options to confirm. You may confirm by phone or by postcard. If your phone number and address are not already in the system, you will probably have to confirm by postcard. If this is the case, it can take up to 6 weeks to receive the postcard, according to the experience of some users.

When confirming by postcard, simply follow the instructions on the card to claim and activate your Google Places page.

Basically, you will log into your Google Places page. You will add your pin number in the appropriate section and then click the go button.

Once you have activated and published your page you're ready to enhance your listing.

BEST PRACTICES

• Use standard capitalization and punctuation, unless your business name or address in the real world contains unusual capitalization and punctuation.

• Use a shared, business email account, if multiple users will be updating your business listing.

• If possible, use an email account with a domain that matches your business URL. For example, if your business website is www.douglife.com, a matching email address would be you@douglife.com.

Chapter 6

Getting the Most From Your Listing

Become a Favorite Place on Google

Is your business listing ranked as a favorite place on Google? The most popular local businesses on Google Places are referred to as Favorite Places. The classification is based on how many Google users looked for additional information about the business.

You might find a Favorite Places sticker from Google displayed at various businesses. Maybe one of them might be your business.

How will people find your business?

Millions of people search for businesses on Google. Your listing will also be available through Google Web Search, Google Maps, Google+, Mobile search, 1-800-GOOG-411 voice directory search, and Google Earth. On any of those services, if someone searches directly for your business name and city, your listing will most likely show up.

Google also displays your listing for searches based on your business category or other related terms.

How can I make the most from my listing on Google?

A rich listing which features a description, several photos, business hours and a link to your website will help encourage potential customers to choose your service.

This extra information can also help Google match your listing to more searches, which might increase the number of views your listing gets.

Posting content on your Google+ Page can also be a great way to increase visibility especially with the introduction of Circles. Many consumers place businesses they frequent into categories that they can view separately when they are interested in your product or service, which gives you a personal level of engagement not found elsewhere on the web.

Google also recommends that you mention your Google listing to current and potential customers. Remind them that they can use Google Maps to find your phone number and address. They can get driving directions to your retail store. They can find the latest coupons; leave a review; and get recent updates.

Why does other information show up in my listing?

Google collects data such as reviews, business hours, photos and more from local directories and various websites and combines this information with what you enter in Google+ Page.

Ranking on Google is completely automated. They cannot manually change the order of individual reviews, even if requested by users.

Google accepts reviews directly from users on Google Maps. If you're concerned about a review that was submitted through Google Maps, click the Flag as inappropriate link found under the review and submit a report. If it's found that the review is in violation of Google Maps policies, they'll remove it.

Some reviews found on Maps listings are created on third-party websites. If you feel that a review from a third-party site is inaccurate, you have to express your concerns to the webmaster of the site where the review was posted. If the review is removed from the third-party website, the change will also be reflected on Google.

Chapter 7

Reviews

In my experience, reviews play an important fact in determining relevance with Google. The more reviews you can get for your business—the better.

But a word of caution...

I've seen people try to fool Google by making up fake reviews for themselves. Understand that Google places "tracking cookies" on your computer and they know who you are and where you are. Even if you log out of one Google account and log back in with another, Google knows that you are one and the same person.

So, don't make the mistakes that many do. Do not review your own business—at least not from any Google account that you have ever used on your computer in the past.

A better way to get reviews for your business quickly is to send an email out to your existing customers and colleagues. Google+ Pages makes this easy. To do this, go to your Google+ page and click on the link that reads, "See your listing on Google Maps." This will take you to your Google Maps listing.

Now, up in the right hand corner of your screen, you will see a picture of the map that depicts your business' physical location. Above that is links to print, email or get a link. If you click "email" a link containing your Google Maps listing will automatically show up in an email.

From here, you can send an email to your past clients, friends, family members or anyone that can give your business a review. They will need a Google Account (Gmail, etc) to do this, but it only takes a few minutes to make a Gmail account and to give you a review. If they already have a Gmail account, it will let them write a review right away.

Here is a sample email that you can send out. You can use this or modify it to suit your needs:

Hi <name>,

(Google Maps link here)

I have recently updated my business information on Google and I would greatly appreciate it if you could visit the above link and write me a review.

If you don't already have a Gmail account, you can set one up in under a minute.

I really appreciate your support!

This should get you some reviews. And with these reviews, your relevance with Google will begin to grow. Remember, the more reviews you can get, the better so be sure not to skip this.

HOW TO RESPOND TO REVIEWS

Before you respond to any customer reviews, it's helpful to read and understand Google's suggestions for responding to reviewers. Here is a link to the guidelines for responding:

http://www.google.com/support/places/bin/answer.py?answer=184271

After you've become a verified Google+ business owner, you can publicly respond to Google Maps reviews on your Place Page.

Here are the instructions for accessing your account to respond to reviews:

1. Log into your Google account that you have claimed as your business listing.

2. Visit your listing's Place Page, and scroll to the reviews section.

3. Click Respond publicly as the owner.

4. Write a response, and then click Publish.

The review will show publicly as a response from the owner.

Chapter 8

Other Google Services

The more data that you have online about your business, the more relevant and established you will appear to Google. In this section, I mention other important services that you should consider when optimizing your Google Places listing.

COUPONS / OFFERS

As the business owner of a Google+ Business Listing, you can offer coupons inside your listing. Users can either print the coupons or use a mobile coupon.

When you add more than just the basic elements to your listing, you're inviting customers to interact with your listing. This will bring you more customers and they will be compelled to write a review or share the listing with one of their friends.

Instructions for Creating a Coupon for Your Listing

To create a coupon, follows these steps:

1. Head over to Google.com/Places and click your listing

2. Click on the Offers tab in the middle right corner of your screen

3. Under the large Google+ Image click "Create an Offer" in Red

4. You'll be taken to a page where you can add information that you want to appear on your coupon. On the right side of the page, a preview of your coupon will update itself as you enter new information.

5. When the preview of your coupon looks the way you want it to look, just click Continue at the bottom of the page.

Your coupon will appear in your business listing within 24 hours. You can find your listing in Google Maps by clicking more info in your listing's info bubble. Then click the Coupons tab.

How to Use a Mobile Coupon

When users search for businesses from their mobile phones, they see your Google+ Pages coupon on their phone. When they visit your business in person, they can show you the coupon on the screen of their mobile device, without having to print it out. Mobile coupons are a great way to save paper and natural resources.

How to Create a Mobile Coupon

We've talked about using a mobile coupon, but you might be wondering how to create one. Once you've created a coupon for your regular business listing, there's nothing special you need to do to create a mobile coupon. They're the same, and the process of creating them is the same.

USER CONTENT

Go to Google.com and click "Maps." Now, for the sake of this example, type in something like "Seattle gyms." On the left side (in the search results), you will see a listing of gyms in Seattle. Click on the "more info" on one of the places listings (look for one with a map marker) and it will take you to that Google Maps page. If you scroll to the bottom of the page, you will see "User Content." User content is information left that users have left in open collaboration. These Google users can add maps, reviews, photos, etc. The important feature here that I want to point out is adding a Map—basically, a map inside the map. I do not suggest you do this with your business Gmail account, however.

This feature will increase your relevance by showing that other people have "mapped" your location, usually indicating it is one of their favorite places. If you are a favorite among many, you will be a favorite to Google as well.

Here's how to add a map:
Go back to Google's Map page and sign in with an account that is not your business account.

Sign-in and click "Maps" then click again "My Maps" then click "Get Started".

What you want to do is create a map containing 'tagged' locations.

You can type in your business name and zip code and it will bring you to your listing.

Click the "Public Map" option then "Save".
Zoom-in the map at the location of your business listing. To add tags, click on the "tag" icon (the blue marker at the top of the map) and drag it to the right location on the map.

A window will appear for you to enter the "Title", type your business name in it. In the "Description" box, you can write any description you want but just be sure to include your business address and phone number just as it appeared in your Google maps listing. Then click "OK".

Your Google Maps listing will now display this user content you just added.

Get your customers, friends and families to do the same. This will help increase your relevance with Google.

PERFORMANCE MONITORING

Inside of every Google Places account, you have a Dashboard which displays important statistics about your site. It can show you the number of "'Impressions" you've had.

This just indicates the number of times your listing has been displayed during a search on Google or in a OneBox result after a regular search from Google.

Statistics are not recorded in real time, however. They're compiled from the previous 30-day period, and are shown with a 48-hour delay.

Chapter 9

Other Important Local Listings

Part of becoming more relevant to Google is by being trusted. Part of being trusted is being listed elsewhere on the Internet on websites that Google trusts.

To start earning this trust, you should begin by adding your business to other listing services in addition to Google. Google will cross-reference your information contained in other listings. When you list your business with other sites, you should include your address, phone number and all other information that is requested. And remember to keep this information consistent as stated earlier in this book, as you want each and every listing to look exactly alike so that Google counts that listing as being you and, in turn, ranks you higher.

Adding your business to other listings will move you up higher in Google's local ranking results.

The websites that are included here are chosen because they are trusted by Google and also because they are FREE. I highly recommend that you register at each of these.

Yahoo

Go to www.local.yahoo.com and scroll to the bottom of the page. Click "Add a Business."

Enter your business information and click "Submit."

Info USA

Register and setup. Click "Add Business Record". Fill in the information required then click "Submit". Select your business classification. Be sure to enter the same information as the one you entered in Google Maps local listing. Click "Submit."

A message is displayed informing you that it will take up tosixty (60) days for the business to get listed.

Remember: the information you include in the other listings should be exactly the same information for each listing or as close to it as possible.

Bing

Go to www.bingbusinessportal.com/BusinessSearch.aspx

Enter your information in the Find Your Listing form to see if you've already been found by Bing. After that, follow the instructions to either create or claim your business listing on Bing.

Yellow Pages.com

Go to http://listings.yellowpages.com. Click "Get your Free Listing Now". Search for your business by entering your phone number. Since it's not yet on the list, you can enter your business information. Click "Continue" button.

Choose the nearest category for your business. Narrow it down to a more specific category if possible. Click "Add Category" for every category that you have chosen. You are allowed up to five categories to add. Click "Continue" button.

Enter additional information as close as the information from the other listings you've created. Enter the "Access Code" then click "Create Listing".
A new page will prompt you to create an account with yellow pages. Enter information and click "Register."

Super Pages

Go to www.supermedia.com and click "Free Business Listing" at the bottom of the page.

Enter your business phone number then click "Search."
It's not yet on the list so click "Continue" button.

Enter your business information. From the "Choose Your Business Category", enter a category then click "Search."

Add all possible categories. There are no limits as to how many categories to add. Click "Continue" button if you're done adding categories.

Select as many products, services or brands that are applicable to your business. Enter your business hours, payment options, additional details, photos and coupon.

Click "Preview". If you like to upgrade for better listing, you have to pay a certain fee. Click "No, Thanks" to continue if you're happy with the free listing.

A page prompts you to create your account. Fill-in the information then click "Sign-in". Enter your account details then click "Continue."

The "Order Page" appears. Just check the "I Accept" button below then click "Complete Order".

The "Order Confirmation" page appears confirming that the list has been added.

Local Eze

Go to www.localeze.com and click "List your Business Today." From there, go to "Sign Up" and enter your business information. LocalEze usually takes a few weeks before you are listed but this is one of my favorite resources.

Navteq

Register at http://mapreporter.navteq.com/. Enter your business address then click "Find". It's not on the list so click "Click to add a draggable place marker on the map". Drag the place marker to your desired location.

Fill-in the "Point of Interest" (POI) information, then click "Submit".

Yelp

Go www.yelp.com and Click "Sign Up For Yelp"

Search for your business name. It's not there so you can now "Add your Business to Yelp". Fill-in your business information like what you did with the other listing services. Click "Submit."

Check your email to verify by clicking on the link provided.

City Search

Go to www.citysearch.com and search for your business name. If it wasn't found then click "Add Business." Enter your business information then click "Submit."

Insider Pages

Go to www.insiderpages.com and search for your business name.

If it wasn't found then click "Add a Business". Click "Join Today" and fill your account and business information.

You can now "Claim this Business."

Other Directories

You can choose from other service listings below that are applicable to your business. The procedure is almost the same when adding a new business. Be sure to enter the exact information as those you have entered from the previous listings.

- http://tripadvisor.com/
- http://gayot.com/
- http://ask.com
- http://guidespot.com
- http://zagats.com
- http://fodors.com/
- http://travelocity.com/
- http://wcities.com/
- http://hotelguide.net/
- http://merchantcircle.om

Submit your business to as many listing services as possible so Google can find many references to your business online. This will give your business a better chance to appear in the local listing.

After listing your business to several services, I recommend that you "social bookmark" all your business listings in each of these directories. Social Bookmarking is a way to publicly share your bookmarked websites and it is another way to make your business become more relevant in Google's eyes.

Start with www.socialmarker.com. Just have a copy of all your business listing URLs and bookmark it in as many social bookmarking sites as possible.

Chapter 10

Geo Target Your Photos

You can further increase your relevance by uploading photos of your business on public photo sharing sites. Specifically, these photos will be placed on maps at your business location.

There are two sites that I recommend and I will walk you through getting started on each.

Panoramio

Go to www.panoramio.com and sign-in (Sign-up for an account if you don't have one). Click "Upload your photos".

Click "Browse" for every photo to be uploaded then click "Upload" at the bottom of the page.

After successfully uploading all the photos, enter the title, tags and comment with your business name, tags and address as it appear in the Google maps listing.

To map the photos, click "Map this Photo" then map it to your business address. Click "Search" beside the address box then

"Zoom" to make sure the photo is in the exact location you want (You can drag it to your desired location if it's not positioned there).

Then click "Save Position."

Repeat the process for all the remaining photos. Once finished mapping the photos, click "Save" at the bottom of page.

Flickr

Go to www.flickr.com. You can either create a new account or you can sign-in with a yahoo account.

Click "Upload Photos & Videos" then click "Choose your Photos & Videos" to pick up photos to be uploaded.

Be sure to click the "Public" option button before hitting the "Upload" button below the page. Click "Add a Description" so you can enter your business name, address and tags the same as it is in the Google Maps Listing. Click "Save."

To map the photos, click a photo then click "Add to your map" on the bottom right pane. Click "OK", choose the "Anyone" option button as your "Default Permission". When your map is displayed, click the dropdown arrow list at the bottom and choose "All your content" to display all your photos. Drag each photo to your targeted location.

Mapping photos on Panoramio or Flickr help by adding more content to your business listing in Google.

You can also Geo Target with webcams which will further add more content and more citations to your Google Places listing. But due to the fact that most businesses do not incorporate webcams, I will not go into the details. If you are interested in pursuing this, however, a good place to start is www.earthcam.com.

Chapter 11

Citations

In traditional SEO, inbound links are critical to ranking well on the search engines. However, with Google's local algorithm—the one that is used to populate Google Places and Google Maps, geographic-related links called citations are used.

In a patent owned by Google: Authoritative Document Identification, Google indicates the importance of physical location and how they tie citations to local businesses (U.S. Patent application #20060149800):

Abstract: A system determines documents that are associated with a location, identifies a group of signals associated with each of the documents, and determines authoritativeness of the documents for the location based on the signals.

The patent information is quite a read, but in there, Google identifies what a document is:

"document," as the term is used herein, is to be broadly interpreted to include any machine-readable and machine-storable work product. A document may include, for example, an e-mail, a web site, a business listing, a file, a combination of files, one or more files with embedded links to other files, a news group posting, a blog, a web advertisement, etc.

What this shows is that a crawl able link is not necessary for your business to receive a citation online. It now appears that a mention of your business online is enough to give you some attention from Google.

But, just like links, it appears that Google still places an importance on where the citation comes from. If a citation comes from the local Chamber of Commerce, it seems to carry more weight than if it comes from your sister's blog (although the blog will still hold some weight because volume is important too).

There are many ways to get your business listed aside from Google maps. The reason why you should get listed in many places as possible is that you achieve more citations.

Citations help make your business popular within search engines. The more citations you have, the more popular your business becomes. SEO calls this link popularity. Google and other search engines take into consideration the number and quality of links you have when it comes to link popularity.

The idea is the same in local search. However, it's not the links that are taken into consideration but instead, the mention of your business name in relation to your business location.

When Google finds that you are listed in other sites with the same business location, "trust" builds up and you become very relevant in its eyes.

Now, what you want to do is start getting your business and its location placed on local websites to increase the amount of citations you have with Google Places/Google Maps.

To do this, you should first do a Google search for business directory websites in your local area. For example, if you are a plumber in Seattle, do a search for "Seattle plumber directory" or "Seattle business directory" etc. From the search results for this term, you should find good ideas to list your website.

In most cases, these types of websites will have a place for you to include your business information. If nothing is available, send them a request through a "contact us" link on the website.

Google will give you some serious credit if you are located on important websites like the Better Business Bureau and your local Chamber of Commerce websites because these are considered authoritative and because they have built-in trust. The drawback, however, is that these are often paid listings, although they are usually well worth the price you pay.

Chapter 12

Advanced Techniques

This section is devoted to bringing you advanced techniques and resources that you might not easily uncover by yourself. These techniques come as a result of more than 14 months of actually working within the system.

To save you time and to help you eliminate frustrations, here is a list that you can refer to after your Google+ Page listing has been functional for about two months.

You might have increased success by utilizing and applying some of these techniques prior to the two-month time frame. However, if you want to increase your ranking, get more new business customers, and make more sales, this is where you will find that information.

In no particular order, here are the insider tips and tricks.

• Often overlooked when creating a new business listing, is the importance of recording your business data into an electronic document. Although this is so simple, most business owners don't do it, and their listings fail miserably.

The secret technique is that every time you list, submit, talk about or mention your business that all your contact information must be presented in the same way. It should match your business name and data that was entered at Google Places. This is especially true for citation resources, directories, and review sites. The search engines love discovering businesses online where all location information matches.

• Buy a domain name that already has pagerank that contains your keyword phrase, and is priced around $50. A seasoned and established domain name that is more than two years old is easier to rank than a brand new domain name that you just bought today.

• Look at other Google Places listings and click on their information page, especially if they are marketing to the same target audience that you are. Especially if they are ranking high for a specific keyword, look to see where their citations and reviews are coming from. You might even want to open up a document file or spreadsheet and record the URLs as places where you can submit your listings to.

• Search for local directories where you live. For example, you would combine your keyword with your city, plus the word "directory." Thus, your search phrase would look like this: fish and chips + Seattle + directory. The search results would return a list of directories in your local area that will be golden and targeted for your business.

• To get your site and your listing ranked faster than four months, create simple social networking sites named with your keyword in the title that openly displays your business name and your business information.

Some sites that have been successful are found at Weebly, HubPages, Squidoo, Facebook, Twitter, and LinkedIn. The goal is to get as many places as possible mentioning your business name, your phone number, your address, your location, and what your specialties are.

• Become a detective to learn more about the businesses who compete with you. How do you do this? Whenever you see a listing on the Internet that's on the first page of Google for Google+ Pages, click through the links such as reviews, and even the section that says "more about this place."

The information you'll find will save you months of research. Are they using 10 photos and five videos to promote their listing? Is their content focused on their keywords? Study listings and become a copycat. Whatever is working for them could work for you, too. Do they have lots of reviews? If so, then that's where you need to spend your time in order to get more reviews and more customers.

• Offer a bonus, a discount, a coupon, a free product, or some other incentive for your customers to leave their review of your business on one of your top review sites. This is a new tactic for online businesses to use. However, off-line retail businesses have been doing this for years.

Have you ever looked at a store receipt and seen that if you call a specific number and rate the service, that you get five dollars off your next purchase? Try it. It works.

• Adding coupons to your listing will improve the number of people who click through to your website take advantage of your cost-saving offer.

• You would be amazed at the tips, tricks, and techniques that are openly discussed on the Google Places help forum. You need to spend about 30 minutes inside the help forum. You will learn so much. In fact, don't make this a one-time experience.

If you truly want to improve your listing and your ranking for your site, do yourself a favor. Put this task on your daily to-do list. There are more secrets and techniques revealed on this forum than you could imagine.

• The latest trend in the past two years and being copied more and more everyday are the companies who offer a daily deal on a product or a service in your local area. Every morning an email arrives with the latest deal. You have 12 hours to purchase the deal of the day. You can use the coupon usually any time within the next 12 months.

Sites such as www.groupon.com, www.livingsocial.com, www.localtwist.com and hundreds more are available for you to participate in. Uniqueness of this type of advertising is that you do not have to spend any money to get your business advertised on any of these services.

The company helps you write the ad, helps you take the photos, and helps you with suggestions on promoting what you are selling. They take a percentage of the total sales, and at the end of the day, they mail you a check for the profits that you made.

The bonus is that you can get hundreds and even thousands of new customers in one day who willingly pay to receive your product or service. And you don't even need a list or a website to get this done.

Do you think advertising your business through this type of service would get your business name, address, and phone number out there?

This technique alone is worth hundreds of dollars. And what if you offered a bonus or special incentive to everyone who left you a review? Do you think your Google Places listing would become popular and rank higher and bring you more traffic and customers than you ever imagined?

I'm so convinced that you can increase your business substantially through Google+ Pages, especially because now you know many of these insider tips and secrets.

Chapter 13

Facebook

I don't think there is an off-page SEO book on the market that does not at least mention Facebook. The fact is, Facebook recently ousted Google as the number one most visited website in 2012. Because of that, Facebook is an important player in any online marketing strategy.

Although Facebook is widely considered to be used for personal chatting between friends and family, it is also a powerful way for businesses to connect more personally with their customers.

Facebook allows for business pages and it is important that you start one for your business. Setting one up is fast, easy and painless.

If you have no personal facebook account yet you have to first sign-up for one before you can setup a facebook business fanpage. Once logged in, enter www.facebook.com/pages in the browser, and then at the top of the page click the "Create a Page" button at the right side of the screen.

Choose the type of page that best suits your business, enter your business page name in the text box provided then click "Create Page."

If you need additional information, check out the facebook help center. The help center has all the information you need about setting up your facebook page.

To enter the basic information about your page, click the "View Page", click the "Info" tab then click the "Edit Information."

Once you have adjusted the settings, you can click "Save Changes." (Be sure to enter your information exactly as it appears in your Google Maps Listing).

Also be sure to add your website and target keyword phrases.

When you are ready to publish your page, simply click "Publish this Page". (You can make additional changes by clicking "Edit Page"). You can now add pictures. Your location should match your Google map listing. The page name should also be the name you have on your Google map listing.

There is so much more you can do with Facebook than these basics, but that's for another book!

Chapter 14

Spying on Your Competition

To get a top ranking in the regular search results, one must have the most number of powerful incoming links. Traditional SEO calls it link popularity and backlinks.

The same works with Google maps. To get to the top, one must have the most number of website citations.

The fastest and easiest way to determine how to beat your competition is by spying on their Google Maps listings and using that information to your advantage. Understand that they are not in the number one position by luck or happenstance. They are there because they are doing something that has made them appear to be more relevant than you in Google's eyes (their local algorithm).

Again, in almost all cases, it is simply the fact that they have more citations than you. But, volume is not always the case. Once again, they may have a few less citations than you, but they may be listed on websites that Google deems more authoritative. But, as a general rule, go after the volume and revise later.

To see where your competition is receiving citations, all you need to do is go to their Google Maps page and scroll down to the category listed as "More about this place." This is where the citations for that business are listed. From here, you can visit these pages where your competitors are listed and try to get your business listed as well.

There are instances wherein a keyword phrase, say "Beverly Hills cosmetic surgery", returns a result when searched in Google although there are only a few citations. What made it to the top? It's because it had more reviews than the other competitors. But if you keep an eye on the status of this keyword phrase everyday you will see that this will not stand in that spot long because it does lacks citations.

There are competitors that stay on the top positions although they don't have that much information like reviews, hours of operations, photos and videos, and other business information. What made them to the number one position? It's because they have the most number of citations listed on the Internet with their business name, business location and business phone number. It is clear that it's these citations that got to them to number 1 position in the results. Bottom line? Go get your citations. Be sure to visit the citations of your competition and get mentioned on the same sites. Once you are listed on all the same sites that your competition is, go get more citations...and keep getting them. Go get more reviews...and keep getting them.

Adding citations and reviews on a regular basis will propel you to the top of Google ...and continuing to work on it will keep the competition at bay. This is how you dominate your competition and garner a ton of website visits, telephone calls and more traffic for your business.

Chapter 15

On Page SEO for Your Website

While off page is more important to Local Search results rankings than on page factors, I think it is very important to devote a short chapter on the basics of on page optimization as it pertains to Local Search results.

On-page optimization should begin just as traditional SEO begins...and that is by building relevance through location + keywords.

Tasteful keyword placement in your website should be considered a high priority and they should be used with a geographic slant if possible.

Additionally, your full business name, address and telephone number should be placed on every page in your website with a link to your Google+ Page.

If you're a blogger (and you should be), it's crucial to verify Authorship with Google+. This feature allows better branding and visibility within search engines.
http://plus.google.com/authorship

There are many places where you can insert your target keyword phrase to optimize your site. It is always recommended that, at minimum, you include the primary target keyword phrase in the title of your website, along with some other key phrases that engage visitors who view your titles and descriptions in search engine results. It is also great if you can work your keyword phrase into your business name but that's not always possible.

For example, if you are a cosmetic dentist, the most likely keyword term used to find you would be, "cosmetic dentist." If you were based in Seattle and your actual business name was Brite Smile Dentistry, you would want to use something similar to: Seattle Cosmetic Dentist, Mark Rogers DDS: Bright Smiles Dentistry. This way, you keyword is placed out in front and used as the business name. And with the example I gave, you could still include your actual business name.

Besides the business name and website title, you should also include your target keyword phrase in your website's headline, main body text, footer, title tag and meta tags.

If you do not know how or have the time to do this yourself, I highly recommend hiring a professional Online Marketing Consultant with SEO experience. They will know exactly what you're looking for and they can take the necessary steps to handle your on-page SEO and get back to your business.

Conclusion

This book is meant to give you a real insight into how to use Google+ Business Pages to gain more exposure for own or your clients business. The information has been presented in a step-by-step process so even if you're completely new to online marketing you can easily follow along.

If you follow the steps and take action, you can watch as your business climbs the ranks of Google Maps to help grow their businesses. Having this information gives you an advantage.

Remember, relevance is the key. Make your business relevant to Google through useful information, reviews, citations and a fully optimized Google+ Business listing and Google will reward you with higher rankings.

See you on the first page of Google ☺!

Epilogue

So now you've reached the end of this book. I would suggest that you read it a second time to let it all sink in as there is quite a bit of information that we've covered. And by applying what you've learned from this book to help you increase your business exposure, I'm glad I was able to help you get closer to your online business goals.

What's Next?

If you follow what I have outlined in this book, you can achieve more traffic within local search results. And if you are looking for more advanced help in improving your online presence or if you would like to have your online marketing managed by a professional, then I'm here to help.

To learn more about my products, services, and get your free consultation, visit www.douglife.com and take the next step! Together we can map out the best strategies that will work for you, and keep you on track to your business goals and success.

Here's to your online success!

Doug Montgomery

NOTE: The internet is ever-growing, ever-evolving and Google is constantly making changes and modifying how they present your local business in their search results. This book reflects my best practices and procedures as they are at this time. I will continually update this information to keep pace with ongoing changes. And I will make these updates available to you.

To receive updates from me on this book, just send an email to doug@douglife.com with "update" in the subject line and I'll keep you informed of changes as they become available.

About The Author

Douglas Montgomery – www.douglife.com

While everyone else played sports and had after-school activities, I spent my time inside learning how to use DOS on my 486. What a prize it was. Since 1996 I have helped hundreds of business owners successfully use the internet to grow their businesses. She is an expert at web design and custom web development, and specializes in helping businesses find creative and innovative ways to "take it to the web".

Doug is a seasoned web designer and experienced web online marketing consultant. He has more than two decades of experience in information technology, senior project management, technology consulting and online website analysis.

Doug is a recognized author, speaker, and teacher in the internet marketing industry - and he enjoys above all helping others achieve success and educate themselves to sustain their business online.

To learn more about how Doug can help you succeed on the web, schedule your free consultation today – www.douglife.com